Finance 102 for Kids

Practical Money Lessons Children Cannot Afford to Miss

Finance 102 for Kids

Practical Money Lessons Children Cannot Afford to Miss

Walter Andal

gatekeeper press™
Columbus, Ohio

Finance 102 for Kids: Practical Money Lessons Children Cannot Afford to Miss

Published by Gatekeeper Press
2167 Stringtown Rd, Suite 109
Columbus, OH 43123-2989
www.GatekeeperPress.com

The cover design for this book is entirely the product of the author. Gatekeeper Press did not participate in and is not responsible for any aspect of this element.

Library of Congress Control Number: 2021932528

ISBN (paperback): 9781662909191
eISBN: 9781662909207

Acknowledgments

I have to start by thanking my loving wife, Anne. From reading the early drafts to providing me with thoughtful and constructive advice, she has always been my rock and my inspiration. From the bottom of my heart, thank you my dearest!

I would like to thank Lisa Rojany of Editorial Services of L.A. for editing the manuscripts and for guiding me throughout the publishing process.

Many thanks to my primary illustrator, Richard Peter David, for his creativity and diligence. It was a pleasure and an honor to work with such a great talent.

I am immensely grateful to Jenniffer Brescini and Joel Cahn for their insights and feedback especially during my research process.

Special thanks to my eldest son, Gabriel Andal, for providing the illustrations to one of the most important concepts in finance: compound interest.

This book is dedicated to our four amazing children. Gabriel, Angelo, Jacob, and TJ, may this book serve as a beacon in your pursuit of success and happiness!

Contents

Introduction:
Welcome to the Class!

Hi! Mr. Buckingham here, welcoming you back to another exciting class on money and finance!

In *Finance 101,* you learned how money started, how it can be earned, why it is important to save, and how to make your money grow. You also gained insights into the benefits and dangers of credit, the basics of the stock market and the economy, and the significance of giving back to the community.

As a review, **finance** is the way money is managed. Money can be earned or made in several ways, like working for someone, starting a business, or investing. Although you can make or earn money, you can also lose it. You might lose money when you overspend, when you make the wrong investments, or when you just don't take good care of it.

Managing money may not be as easy as you think. Many people make poor decisions with their money. Some people spend all the money they make. Not having enough savings in times of need can cause a lot of stress. It can be scary when you don't have money to pay for basic needs such as food, clothing, housing, and education. Some people lose their house, car, and personal belongings when they run out of money. If you don't have enough money to pay for your basic needs, it will be even more challenging to get other things you might consider essential in today's environment, such as cell phones, computers, books, and internet service.

Similar to how you develop your math, music, or athletic skills, developing money skills requires ongoing learning and practice. A skill cannot be acquired in just one sitting. You have to keep on reading and learning, asking people for guidance and advice, and practicing what you learn. You might make mistakes as you start to deal with money, and that is okay as long as you are learning from those experiences. What is important is that you are developing your financial skills one step at a time, and you are enhancing them as you grow older and smarter.

And so, welcome to ***Finance 102***! This is a class where you will learn one useful money lesson at a time, and you can use these lessons to build up and develop valuable skills. With patience and an open mind, you can apply the lessons from this class to help you gain the skills needed to make smart choices with your money. Remember that what you do today with your money will have a huge impact on your future.

Are you ready to learn more? Let the learning (and the fun) begin!

LESSONS ON SPENDING WISELY

Lesson #1:
Live within Your Means

The idea of "living within your means" is one of the best ways you can manage your money. This concept means spending no more than the money you have. When you choose to live within your means, you are limiting your expenses to less than what you have or what you are going to make. In other words, you are not overspending.

You might be asking, "How can someone spend more than what he or she has?" Remember, in *Finance 101* we learned about the power of credit cards and other modes of borrowing money, such as student loans and car loans. With a credit card, you can buy something immediately even without any money on hand. Credit cards are useful when you have an emergency or when you must buy something you really need. However, the big challenge when people have access to credit cards is that it allows them to buy more than what they can afford. People can easily spend without thinking whether or not they can pay back what they owe. Sometimes, people underestimate the dangers of making many unnecessary purchases with their credit cards until they can no longer afford to pay off and manage their debts.

Living within your means does not mean living cheaply or depriving yourself of good stuff. You have the freedom to choose how to use the money you receive or earn. However, you are responsible to know what you can afford. Any person can still live a good and modest life by making wise choices with their money. You may not be able to get all the things you want now, but you can still make fewer yet smarter purchases while also saving some of your money for future use. Sometimes, it takes planning and some degree of discipline and patience to make things work, so you can enjoy the money you have without putting a burden of debt on yourself.

Lesson #2:
Know the Difference between a Need and a Want

Have you thought about the difference between a **need** and a **want**? A **need** is something that you must have in order to live, while a **want** is something that would make you happy, comfortable, or excited, but you can actually live without. Needs are easier to identify because those are the things necessary to survive. You have basic needs, such as food and water, a place to live, and clothing. Nowadays, some people consider education as a need. This is because a good education can provide the knowledge and skills that can significantly help anyone become more successful in life.

Sometimes it can be difficult to draw the line between a need and a want. For example, clothing is a need as it protects and warms the body, but a $100 brand-name shirt or a $200 pair of designer jeans may not be a real need. Likewise, needs and wants can also vary from person to person. A top-of-the-line pair of running shoes may be a need for a professional athlete, but that same pair of shoes may be a want for a typical student.

To help you determine whether an item is a need or a want, ask yourself these three questions before buying. If you answer yes to any of the questions, the item you are looking at is most likely a want.

Knowing the difference between a need and a want is useful in managing your money. It can help you make better choices with your money and avoid unnecessary spending. If you can figure out that an item you hope to purchase is a want, you can pause before you pay and reevaluate whether you should buy it now, buy it at a later time, or refrain from buying at all. You have little to lose and a lot to gain when you can say no to things that fall under the want category.

Bear in mind that there is nothing wrong with buying things that you truly want. You are entitled to enjoy the money you earn. Yet by not giving in to all your wants or desires, you are gaining self-control and power over your money. Though you are still young, and you might feel there is no pressing need to save, you will be ahead of the game when you are able to prepare early for more important things that you have to purchase at some point in the future, such as a higher education, a car to take you to work, and a house to shelter you and your future family.

Lesson #3:
Create and Follow a Simple Budget

A **budget** is a written spending and saving plan over a period of time. A period of time can be weekly, monthly, or yearly. Having a budget enables you to see how much money you expect to earn or receive, how much you can spend on different items or categories, and how much you can set aside for savings. When you have a budget, you can determine if you have enough money to buy all the things you need and want.

Having a budget is very helpful, but many people resist making a budget because of the misconception that doing so is a time-consuming hassle. Some also think that they are too poor to make a budget. However, making a budget is very important no matter how much money you have because a budget can bring order to your finances.

There are many benefits that come from having a budget. First, a budget prevents overspending. When you make a budget, you carefully identify the items or categories where you intend to use your money. If you follow a budget, it makes it easier to resist buying unnecessary things that are not listed in your written plan.

Second, a budget enables you to prioritize your spending. To **prioritize** means to decide which things are more important to you. When you prioritize your spending, you consider the different items you want to have and figure out which will take precedence or higher priority in your budget. Given the limited amount of money you can expect to receive, having a budget allows you to make trade-offs and spend your money on the items you consider as higher priorities. By prioritizing, you are able to use your money for things that make more sense to you and make you happy without putting yourself in financial trouble.

Third, having a budget gives you some flexibility with your spending. When you make a budget, you decide how much you will spend on different categories such as food, clothing, school supplies, and entertainment activities. The good thing about this is that you can make adjustments as long as you are meeting your overall goals. For example, if you want to go out to a movie with your friends on the weekend, you might want to lessen your spending on other categories for the next few days so you can have more money available for hanging out with your friends.

Last but not least, having a budget gives you a game plan on how you can buy an expensive item that you want at some point in the future. If you want to get a powerful laptop, or you would like to watch a live game of your favorite professional sports team, then you can put more of your money toward a fund that you can use later for that particular big expense. The more money you can set aside, the faster you can reach your goal of getting the item you want.

Ben's Monthly Budget

MONEY COMING IN (INCOME)	
Earnings from Babysitting	$ 80
Monthly Allowance ($10/week x 4)	40
Total Monthly Income	$120
MONEY GOING OUT *(EXPENSES)*	
Food ($15/week x 4)	60
Drinks ($2/week x 4)	8
School Supplies	7
New Shirt	12
Subtotal Monthly Expenses	87
Donation to Charity	3
Total Monthly Expenses and Donations	$90
Amount Saved for the Month	$30

Look at Ben's monthly budget. Ben estimates that he will make $120 this month. He plans to use $87 of his money toward food, drinks, school supplies, and clothing. He also sets aside $3 for a charity donation. At the end of the month, he expects to save $30. As you can see, a budget allows Ben to control and prioritize his spending, determine how he wants to spend his money, and save a portion for his future use.

Lesson #4:
Minimize Impulse Buying

Impulse buying happens when someone makes a purchase without planning and without considering the consequences of the purchase. Impulse buying is driven by emotions and feelings. A lot of people buy impulsively to quickly satisfy a need or a desire. Some shoppers get excited and buy impulsively when they see something on sale. There are also people who shop impulsively when they get sad or stressed out because shopping makes them happy or helps them unwind.

Impulse buying can range anywhere from small items, such as a candy, a box of chocolates, or a toy, to more expensive items, such as a pair of shoes, a smartphone, a high-end TV, or even a car. Buying on impulse can put someone in financial trouble, especially when it takes away money that is set aside for essential purchases.

Once in a while, it is okay to buy on impulse as long as the purchase is for a low-cost, high-reward item. For example, you treated yourself with a candy or cookie in a checkout line, or you went out to a movie with friends after a grueling exam. Nevertheless, you cannot be impulsive when dealing with large purchases such as a smartphone, jewelry, or a car. Expensive items bought on impulse are most likely unnecessary purchases, and this behavior can easily ruin your finances.

Sometimes, it is very difficult to resist impulse buying, especially when it involves a low-cost, high-reward item. To be ready for such spending, some people put a small amount of money in their budget for "miscellaneous expenses" in case they need to make an unplanned or impulse purchase. By doing so, it allows you to satisfy some of your cravings without causing a huge dent in your budget.

LESSONS ON COST AND PRICE

Lesson #5:
Research and Compare Prices

The prices of the goods and services you buy can differ from one store to another. Sometimes, even prices of identical items in the same neighborhood will be different. There are many reasons why prices vary. Some stores set the prices of their products higher because they may be offering more benefits and perks for their customers, such as better customer service, cleaner and more organized stores, better product selection, or more lenient return and exchange policies. On the other hand, there are many stores that choose to sell their goods at a lower price because they keep their business expenses low, and, in return, they pass the savings to the shoppers. Some stores set their prices lower to aggressively compete with neighboring stores.

Because the prices of identical or similar products may differ, you can save money by comparing prices before you buy, especially when buying expensive items or the things you purchase frequently. To determine whether the price is on the high side or low side, you have to do research and comparison shop. **Comparison shopping** is the practice of comparing the price of products or services from different vendors before buying.

The internet makes it convenient to do comparison shopping. When you compare prices online, you can see the prices at different online vendors, and possibly even the prices at some local stores. Comparison shopping is very useful, especially when you are planning to buy expensive items such as smartphones and computers. By paying attention to the price differences, you can wisely choose to spend your money at stores that can give you the most value for your money.

When shopping online, you need to consider the cost of shipping, as this can make the final cost higher compared with the original price you saw. Several online vendors offer free shipping when you reach a certain amount in your shopping cart. Some vendors also offer free shipping when the product is shipped to their local stores, where you pick up the item. Stay away from online vendors who charge "handling fees." They will tempt you with a low price but will charge you extra in the form of handling fees. With shipping and/or handling fees, you may end up paying more than the item costs from another vendor.

When buying household goods and grocery items, you may notice that many products are packed in different sizes and are priced differently. The best way to determine which gives you the most value is to compare the unit price, which is the price per unit of measurement, such as ounces, pounds, grams, or liters. Large sizes often have a lower unit price, which means you are getting more value for your money. However, before buying in bulk or large sizes, you have to make sure that you will use all of the contents before the expiration date.

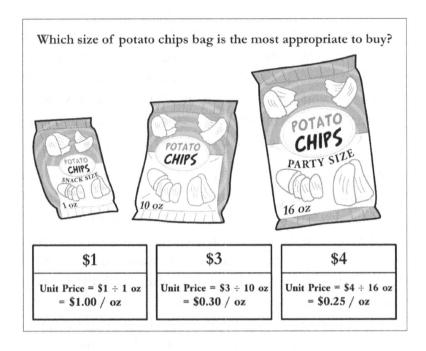

Which size of potato chips bag is the most appropriate to buy?

$1	$3	$4
Unit Price = $1 ÷ 1 oz = $1.00 / oz	Unit Price = $3 ÷ 10 oz = $0.30 / oz	Unit Price = $4 ÷ 16 oz = $0.25 / oz

Although the "party size" bag gives you the most value for your money, the most appropriate bag to purchase really depends on your need. If you want to grab a quick snack to satisfy your hunger, or you simply want to taste the flavor, then the $1 "snack size" may work well for you. However, if you love eating potato chips, or you would like to share this with your family or friends, then buying the biggest bag will make the most sense.

Lesson #6:
Everyone Pays Taxes

When you buy an item in a store, you may notice that the amount you pay differs from the original price tag. This is because you and everyone else have to pay tax. A **tax** is the money that people and businesses pay to the government. The government collects taxes in order to pay for the services that it provides to the public, including education, healthcare, recreation, and security. The government uses income from taxes to pay the people who work for the government as well as pay for infrastructure projects, such as roads, bridges, hospitals, schools, and libraries. Tax income is also used to maintain the order and cleanliness of streets, parks, beaches, and other public areas.

The government collects taxes from people and businesses in many ways. When someone earns money from a job or a business, the government will collect **income tax**. Owners of fixed properties like houses, land, and buildings pay **property tax**. When people buy certain goods and services, such as books, cars, or phone and internet subscriptions, the government charges **sales tax** to the buyers.

As you have to pay sales tax on almost every purchase you will make, you have to consider the extra money that you will need to pay, especially when planning for a large purchase. Even though you might have saved enough money to buy an item you want, it may not be enough to pay for the total cost of the purchase including taxes.

As you get older and start to earn more money, you can anticipate that you won't be receiving the full amount of money you earned because you have to pay income tax to the government. If you are working for a company, your employer will likely withhold or take out a certain portion of your salary to pay for your income tax. The employer will send that money to the government as your income tax payment. If you are self-employed, which means you own a business or you are working independently for yourself, you have to set aside a certain portion of your earnings to pay for the tax at the end of the year. Not paying income tax will land you in big trouble with the government.

Lesson #7:
Consider the Total Cost of Ownership Prior to a Big Purchase

There are personal devices, gadgets, and machines that may cost you extra to make them work. These include video game consoles, cell phones, computers, and cars. On top of the taxes, some of the additional expenses you may encounter include gas, electricity, service/subscription fees, insurance, maintenance, and repairs. To illustrate this, let us explore the true cost of owning a cell phone and a car.

A cell phone will only be useful when it is able to send and receive calls and messages as well as access the internet. When there is free wireless network available, you can use your cell phone to connect to the internet with no additional costs. But outside of the free wireless network area, you won't be able to connect to the internet unless you subscribe to a phone or internet service.

The cost of subscribing to a phone/internet service varies from one phone carrier to another and also according to the plan you choose. The more minutes, data, and features you include in the plan, the more expensive it gets. The phone service plan can range anywhere from $10 to $100 per month or more. Suppose you get a basic phone plan at $20/month. This means you will spend $240 yearly (12 months x $20) to pay for your phone service. So even if you can buy a phone at a good price, you need to know the cost of subscribing to a phone and internet service, as this will have an impact on your budget.

Buying a car is way more complicated than buying a cell phone. A person who is thinking of buying a car needs to seriously consider the additional expenses and responsibilities associated with operating and maintaining a car. First, there are taxes and other costs to pay on top of the vehicle's price tag. Then, to operate a vehicle, you need to buy gas (or pay for electricity for electric cars). The more you use the car, the more gas you need. When you drive to school or to work, you may need to pay for parking. The car also needs to be registered to the government, and you have to pay for a yearly registration. To keep your car in good shape and safe condition, you will have to bring the car to a shop for a regular oil change and air filter change. Sometimes, a car breaks down, so you may need to buy new parts and pay a mechanic for the repair. Every couple of years, you will also need to buy new tires.

If you obtain a loan to buy a car, the bank will charge you interest on the money you borrowed. Also, both the bank and the government will require you to purchase auto insurance. **Insurance** is a financial tool that can help people manage risks and losses. There are many types of insurance, like home insurance, health insurance, life insurance, and auto insurance. Auto insurance helps you financially when bad things happen to your car, such as when you are involved in a collision or when someone burglarizes or vandalizes your car. When a driver is involved in an accident, the insurance company can pay for the cost of repairing the car and also pay for the damages and problems caused to another vehicle, person, or other properties. However, the insurance is not free. The cost of insurance can be huge, especially for a young person who does not have a long history of good driving or for someone who is reckless and has a bad driving record.

Total Monthly Cost: $450

As you can see, the total cost of owning a car is way more than just the car's price tag or the monthly payments to pay off your car. Recognizing the true cost of ownership can help you create a more accurate and realistic budget. Knowing the extra expenses you need to pay allows you to better prepare for them. If the total cost of owning a car will cause a big burden, then you may consider waiting and saving more until you have enough savings to cover all expenses. What if there is a pressing need to buy a vehicle, but you determine that the true cost will be difficult to manage? Then you may consider looking at much less expensive vehicles, for which your monthly car payments will be more affordable.

Total Monthly Cost: $280

Lesson #8:
The Price Is High
When Demand Is High

Do you remember the lessons on demand and supply from *Finance 101*? To review, the prices of goods tend to go up when there is high **demand** and the supply cannot catch up. On the other hand, the price may go down when the demand weakens or when there is an abundant **supply** of goods available in the market. Let's look at two scenarios to illustrate how a change in demand and supply can cause a change in price.

When the coronavirus hit the world in early 2020, the prices of protective equipment, such as masks and gloves, and household supplies, like hand sanitizers and toilet paper, soared because people were stocking up on these items in large quantities out of fear of them running out at stores. Interestingly, even the prices of gaming consoles, such as Nintendo Switch, rose during the pandemic. Because many families were stuck at home, parents looked for ways to keep the family entertained, and video games provided a good source of entertainment. Similarly, the supply of many products around the world, including gaming consoles, was disrupted because many factories had to temporarily cease their operations during the pandemic. Eventually, when the situation stabilized, the prices of these goods moved back close to their pre-pandemic levels.

Another good example is the case of the iPhone 8. When the iPhone 8 was released in 2017, it sold for nearly $700. The demand was very high, and many loyal iPhone users lined up early in front of stores the day it was released. Eventually, the demand slowed down. By 2018, many people were able to buy an iPhone 8 for $600. In 2019, the iPhone 11 was released, and the demand for the iPhone 8 went down further because many people were buying the latest version instead. By that time, the price of the iPhone 8 dropped to $450, which means a $250 reduction from its initial price. Although newer versions were available, the iPhone 8 was still considered a decent and technologically superior phone in 2019.

When the price of an item is high due to high demand, it may make sense to wait or to find a comparable alternative that is more affordable. This is especially true when there is no pressing need to immediately purchase that high-demand item. Although there are situations where you don't have much choice but to buy it, there might also be many instances where you can save money by patiently waiting a little longer before making that purchase or by considering other less expensive alternatives.

Lessons from the Pro

"Being a smart shopper is the first step to getting rich."

Mark Cuban
Entrepreneur/Investor

Lesson #9:
Avoid Buying Items Priced at a Premium

There are stores that sell their products at a **premium**. An item priced at a premium means the price is higher than normal. Those stores price their goods higher because of the extra benefits that they provide to the customers by virtue of their strategic locations. These types of stores include convenience stores, airport stores, movie theater concession counters, souvenir shops, and vending machines.

A convenience store is a small retail shop that sells everyday items such as food, drinks, groceries, household items, medicine, toiletries, and magazines. Convenience stores are usually located in highly visible areas with easy access and good parking. Customers can park easily and buy the items they need quickly. Many convenience stores are found alongside gas stations. Often, convenience stores are open twenty-four hours a day, which means people can shop inside the stores even in the middle of the night. Many people are willing to pay premium prices at convenience stores because convenience and easy access are important to them.

If you have been in an airport, you might notice that everything is more expensive inside. Airport stores price their products higher because it is more expensive to operate a business inside an airport. The advantage for those stores is that they have a captive audience of airline passengers who do not have any alternatives but to buy the things they need from the airport stores while they are waiting for their flights.

You might also notice that popcorn, water, soda, candy, and snacks are very expensive inside movie theaters. You could be paying more for a snack and a drink inside a movie theater than what you paid for the ticket. Some moviegoers buy only the ticket, but some moviegoers see the value of buying popcorn, snacks, and soda even at a high premium because they want to fully enjoy their movie experience.

Many people are willing to pay extra to enjoy the conveniences provided by these stores. However, your money will buy less when you spend it in stores that sell items at a premium. If you can hold off on your urges to spend your money while inside a movie theater, a convenience store, or the airport, you will be able to pay less when you shop in a regular store.

LESSONS ON STRETCHING YOUR MONEY'S WORTH

Lesson #10:
Use Coupons and Promotional Codes

A **coupon** is a ticket or a document that can be used to get a discount when making a purchase. Coupons are issued by stores and manufacturers and are distributed through mail, newspapers, magazines, and marketing flyers. Some coupons can also be downloaded from retailer and manufacturer websites. The coupon will tell you how much of a discount you will get when you buy a specific item. When you bring a coupon with you to a store, you have to present it to the cashier before making the payment, and the cashier will apply the discount noted on the coupon.

Coupons are issued by retailers to lure customers into their stores. Coupons can also be issued by the manufacturers, and their goal is to attract customers to try their products. Most coupons have an expiration date after which the coupons are no longer valid or accepted.

A **promotional code**, also called a discount code, coupon code, or promo code, is a computer-generated code made up of numbers and letters that can be used to get discounts or perks (like free shipping) when making an online purchase. The concept is very similar to paper coupons. The shopper has to present the discount code (by inputting the code into the promo code box) prior to making the online payment.

Promo codes can be obtained whenever you have access to the internet. A shopper can use search engines to find a promo code. Many bloggers and chat forums also share promo codes through their social network. Sometimes, promo codes can be obtained by registering at the store or manufacturer websites. Although you may sometimes get invalid promo codes, it may still be worth the effort to check and see if the promo codes will provide you some savings before hitting the buy button.

Using coupons and promo codes has its own advantages and disadvantages. On the positive side, shoppers can immediately see significant savings on their purchases. On the flipside, coupons can tempt you to buy items that you don't need. If you have coupons in your hand or in your smartphone, you might think that you don't want to pass on an opportunity to buy an item at a discount, even though there is no need for it. In order to make the coupons truly work for you and save you money, use the coupons only for items that you normally buy or for something that you have been planning to purchase.

Some people don't use paper coupons because they think that using coupons makes them look cheap. On the contrary, coupons actually make any shopper a smart spender. Any money you save using coupons or promo codes means you have more money that you can add to your savings. You don't have to use coupons for all your purchases, but whenever a coupon is available for things you need to buy, it is worth using it. Any savings you make on a purchase you have to make anyway is much better than no savings at all.

Lesson #11:
It's Okay to Inquire about Special Deals and Discounts

From time to time, different stores will offer **discounts** or **special deals** to promote their products or services. Clothing retailers typically do promotional sales when seasons change or when the newer styles of clothes come in. Similarly, fast-food chains and restaurants offer value deals and discounts to attract price-conscious customers. Quite often, they also give special discounts to students.

When shopping for an electronic gadget like a cell phone or a tablet, you may save some money by considering the previous model. To move their inventories, electronics stores offer discounts on older models when newer versions come in. Interestingly, some of the changes or improvements on the newer models may not be that significant or may not mean a lot to you. The older models could be as good as the newer models but cost less. In fact, buying the previous model has one big advantage: It has been tried and tested by thousands of consumers, and shoppers can easily read online reviews on those products.

Many stores make their promotions and special deals visible inside and outside of the store. However, there are also times when the promotional signs aren't obvious. It's also possible that the promotional signs might have been taken down too early before the promotional period is over. In some instances, the promotions are spread only by word of mouth.

When you go into a store, it is okay to inquire for deals, promotions, or available discounts. Often, the store personnel will give you information about their current promotions and special deals, especially when you ask them politely. If the store has nothing special going on, they might tell you about their upcoming sales or promotions. Even if they say no, remember that you have nothing to lose when you inquire. If the store happens to have a great deal that works well for you, it is your lucky day! You are stretching your money's worth when you are able to get good information on any promotions and special deals.

Lesson #12:
Don't Buy Just Because
It Is "On Sale"

You have probably seen local and online stores flashing signs and banners that say Up to 50% off, Buy 1 Get 1 Free, or Clearance Sale. Sales and promotions like these can be very appealing to many shoppers, and some people may see this as a great buying opportunity that they don't want to miss.

Shopping can be an exciting experience, especially when you can buy goods at a reduced price. However, when someone gets too excited by sales and promotions, the person might get tempted to buy things that he or she does not really need or even want. Even though there is a sale, a discount on an item that you don't need is not really a good deal for you no matter how much of a discount you received.

If the item that is on sale is already part of your spending plan, then you should consider buying it. Likewise, if you know that the items on sale are ones you will need later on, you can certainly take advantage of the opportunity to save. For example, when your school backpack is starting to break apart, and a store is offering huge discounts on school backpacks, it may be worth it to check the bags on sale. You can buy the bag now when you find a good one at a discount, and then use it when your old bag is no longer usable.

Spending money on unnecessary things is not a smart decision. If you did not find something that you need during a sales event and you were not able to buy anything, you should not feel bad about it. Rather than pushing yourself to get a sale item that you're not sure you really want or need, it is much better to simply save your money. When you don't spend, you are saving 100 percent of your money. This beats all the promotional deals and sales you will ever find. Your money can always wait for the next sales event, when you can still get a good deal that suits your needs.

Lesson #13:
You Can Get Great Deals on Used and Refurbished Items

There are many things that you should buy new, like shoes and sports safety gear, but there are also a few items that you can just as well buy **used** or refurbished at a price that is much lower than new ones. Some of the things you can buy used include video games, furniture, hand tools, and books. Besides saving money, you are also helping the environment by reusing those items and keeping them out of trashcans and landfills.

The challenge with buying used items is making sure that the item is in good condition and still relevant or up-to-date. Often, buying a used item is a final sale, which means the customer cannot do a return or make an exchange. When buying a used item online, it is a good idea to check the reputation of the seller. Most apps and reselling websites allow the buyers and sellers to rate their experiences after the transaction. You should avoid buying from websites or resellers with bad reviews. Chances are, the items they are selling are of poor quality, or they may be giving you inaccurate information.

When you go to college, one of the expenses you have to prepare for is books. Unfortunately, some publishers will release newer editions to make the previous edition look outdated even though not much was added to the latest book. The good news is that many instructors allow the use of the older edition. In this case, it is better to buy the older used book and use the savings you can get for other college-related expenses.

Refurbished items are products that have been returned to the store. There are many reasons why an item is returned. It could be that the item did not meet the expectations of the buyers. It is also possible that the packaging might have been damaged during the delivery process, or the buyers just changed their minds. Before the store resells the returned items, the store or the manufacturer has to test the item, make any repairs needed, and for most electronics, reset the software to its factory settings. The item will be thoroughly cleaned and repackaged. In most instances, the refurbished item is as good as new, and it is offered at a reduced price.

When shopping for electronic items, such as cell phones, TVs, laptops, and tablets, you may want to compare the prices of brand new versus refurbished items. If there is a huge difference in the price, you may want to consider getting the refurbished one. Also, you should buy refurbished items only from reputable stores that offer either a warranty or a return and exchange program. When the store provides a warranty or is willing to take back refurbished items, the store is most likely vouching for the quality of the refurbished product.

Lessons from the Pro

"Being frugal does not mean being cheap! It means being economical and avoiding waste."

Catherine Pulsifer
Author

Lesson #14:
Avoid Unnecessary Upgrades

Manufacturers will continue to transform and improve their products. They will release newer versions to keep up with the competition and to sell more of their products. For example, you have probably seen many cell phone ads that promote more advanced features such as faster speed, higher resolutions, sleeker design, better security capabilities, bigger memory, or more camera lenses.

As technology continues to improve, many people feel the need to keep up with the changes. When the manufacturers release newer versions of their products, some consumers feel pressured to make an upgrade. However, upgrading your electronic gadgets when a newer version comes out may not always be necessary. As long as your phone works well for you, and its features and capabilities meet your needs, then there is probably no need to upgrade. Avoiding unnecessary upgrades will allow you to save more money today, and you can use your savings when the right time comes for an upgrade.

As you get older, there will be several personal and household items that you will need to eventually replace or upgrade. For instance, your car, air conditioner, washing machine, and television, will break down sooner or later, and the costs for repairs and maintenance can get hefty. They may also become inefficient in regard to electricity or fuel consumption. There will come a time when it will make better financial sense to give up the old item and replace it with something that is better and more efficient. Once you get to that point, you have to research all your options and, if possible, get some advice from trusted people who can help you make the right choice.

LESSONS ON MEDIA AND SOCIAL INFLUENCE

Lesson #15:
Be Aware of the Different Marketing Tactics to Make You Spend

People are constantly bombarded with advertisements. When you turn on the television, you will see different TV commercials. When you access the internet, pop-up ads may interrupt your browsing experience. Your home will receive lots of marketing flyers, letters, and postcards by mail. Newspapers and magazines are filled with hundreds of ads and promotional announcements. Marketers also use billboards to get the attention of commuters. When you visit a shopping mall or a grocery store, you cannot miss the different banners and promotional signs.

Businesses spend lots of money on various marketing tactics. These are used to get your attention, to entice you to try their products or services, to develop brand loyalty, and to make you spend more. Marketing is an important aspect of their business activities in order to sell their products.

Although advertisements can provide you with more information on the different products and services that are available to you, ads can also compel or tempt you to buy things that you may not need. Recognizing and understanding the different marketing tactics can empower you to resist the temptation of an untimely or unplanned purchase.

Here are some of the marketing techniques and tricks used by different businesses to get you to spend more.

- Stores use big SALE signs. This technique is used to bring people inside the stores and get them to make unplanned purchases.

- Marketers create a sense of urgency with their promotions. The ads may say that the promotion is only for a limited time or that the stock is limited.

Doing so puts a little pressure onto the consumers to purchase before time or stock runs out.

- Many stores place essential items, like milk and eggs, at the back of the store. Occasionally, stores also rearrange the store layout. This is to force the shoppers to make their way through the stores and to make them wander around the store longer looking for the items they need. When shoppers stay inside the store longer and see more items, they will likely buy more things than they originally planned for.

- The checkout aisles are stocked with small items to entice shoppers to make a last-minute purchase or to stimulate impulse buying.

- Big companies hire famous people and celebrities to promote and endorse their products. Because of their popularity and influence, an endorsement from a celebrity motivates their fans or followers to purchase the endorsed items.

- Companies pay to get their products featured in movies, television shows, and video games. You might see the main characters in the movie wearing a particular type of shoe or using a certain brand of clothing or car. This is called **product placement**. It is a subtle way to get the audience to develop a positive feeling toward a certain product and make the audience remember the featured product when making a purchase.

Advertisements and other types of marketing promotions can help you get more information about products and services that are available to you. The more information you have, the better decisions you'll be able to make. Ads may also introduce you to new products that you may be unaware of, and they can lead you to great deals on things that you are looking for. However, ads can tempt you into spending on things you don't need or even want. That is why you need to recognize them early and not let advertisements or any other marketing tactics manipulate your buying and saving decisions.

Lesson #16:
On Brand Names vs. Generics, Choose the One that Makes Sense to You

People buy brand-name products for different reasons. Many people associate brand names with high quality. Others prefer brand-name products because of the good experiences they had after using them. Some people buy brand-name products to portray a certain status or to fit into a social circle.

The manufacturers of brand-name products spend a lot on advertisements, endorsements, and packaging to make their products popular and to make them appear superior and unique. Because of the huge investments in marketing and promotions, they have to sell their brand-name products at a higher price. Also, pricing the brand-name products higher sets them apart from competition, as many people associate high price with better quality.

On the other hand, **generics** are products that are basically similar to the branded items but are seldom advertised. They may come in packages that are not as impressive as the brand-name products. Because the manufacturers do not spend as much on ads and packaging, generic products are usually priced lower than brand-name ones.

Although brand-name products are generally considered to have better quality, this does not mean that buying them is always the smarter choice. Many less popular brands or generic products are of similar or comparable quality. A consumer may get the same benefits from using many of the generic products available without the high price tags.

Interestingly, some brand-name companies also make generic versions of their own products to capture shoppers who do not want to splurge on brand-name items. They either repackage the same product or produce a different version. Then they price it competitively to connect with price-sensitive shoppers.

People have different preferences and perceptions, and there is nothing wrong with buying brand-name items. However, a consumer can save money by considering the less expensive alternatives to high-end, brand-name products. If you are open to using comparable and less expensive alternatives, you might be able to buy more with your money or put more money into your savings.

Lesson #17:
Resist Negative Peer Pressure

ANDREW! ANDREW! ANDREW!

Peer pressure is the feeling that you must do the same thing your peers are doing or conform to their expectations. Peer pressure can be a positive or a negative influence. When your friend who excels at school is encouraging you to study harder and be more focused on your goals, you are experiencing positive peer pressure. On the other hand, if you skip classes or drink alcohol because many of your friends are doing it, peer pressure is influencing you negatively. Most kids give in to peer pressure because they want to fit in and avoid being rejected or humiliated by their peers.

Peer pressure can strongly impact the way you manage your money. Because of peer pressure, you might feel compelled to buy a certain brand of clothing or an expensive electronic gadget just to blend in. You might feel pressured by friends to hang out with them at the malls or parties to avoid becoming the odd one out. However, giving in to this type of pressure can push you back from reaching your goals, and it might even get you into financial trouble. You could be buying something you don't need to make your peers like you. You might be using your savings that is allotted for important future use.

It is tough to resist negative peer pressure, especially when you have been with your friends for a long time. However, you need to say no to your peers when they pressure you to act inappropriately. Sometimes, you might even have to stay away from those who are influencing you negatively. If you are facing difficulty with handling negative peer pressure, you should speak with your parents or a counselor. They can help you feel better and also provide you the support you need to resist the negative peer pressure.

Better yet, you can be the person who will positively influence your peers. Try to win over one peer at time to do what is right, especially with their money. When there are enough kids acting positively together, peers are able to pressure each other into doing good deeds and making smart choices.

Friends are supposed help each other grow and become better people. A real friend will not put you in a bad situation, nor will they feel good when you get in trouble. It may be tough, but you can be a good role model to your friends. If you see your friends overspending, show that you care by reminding them to use their money wisely. You don't have to monitor their spending habits, nor control their spending. But by showing your friends that you care by encouraging them to become better money managers, you are helping them succeed. You are also earning their trust and respect.

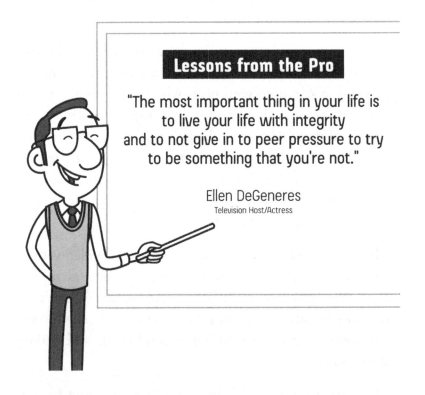

Lessons from the Pro

"The most important thing in your life is to live your life with integrity and to not give in to peer pressure to try to be something that you're not."

Ellen DeGeneres
Television Host/Actress

Lesson #18:
Keeping Up with Your Neighbors Is a Losing Battle

Many of your neighbors or friends may be living in bigger houses, getting dropped off at school in expensive cars, or enjoying fancier gadgets and clothing than you do. There may be times when you feel envious to see them having better and more expensive stuff. Sometimes, this bothers you and makes you want to get the same or even much better items. Because of this, you might have asked your parents to buy you the top-of-the-line running shoe, an expensive pair of designer jeans, or a new smartphone similar to what your friends have. Or you might have used your savings to buy a fancy item because you wanted to keep up with your friends and neighbors.

Unfortunately, trying to keep up with your neighbors or friends is a losing battle. This is because every time you get close to being on top, someone can set the bar higher by getting something better. Even when you buy the latest smartphone or electronic device, a newer one will come out shortly, and you might then start to think that your device has become outdated because one of your peers has bought the newer model.

Comparing what you have with the belongings of your neighbors or peers can make you unhappy and resentful. But you really don't know what is going on with their family's financial situation. Their parents may be successful with their careers or businesses, and they can truly afford to buy expensive items. However, some of them may be living beyond their means and cannot really afford the extravagant lifestyle. They may be overusing their credit cards or drowning in other debts, or they may not be saving enough to prepare for any emergencies or other future needs.

You should avoid comparing what you have with others because you and your family might have different financial goals and priorities. Even if your parents make the same income as those families who spend more, it is possible that your parents don't want to splurge on expensive items that your family does not need. People have different priorities, and theirs might be to give you more opportunities to participate in enriching activities like sports and traveling. It might also be your parents' priority to save for your college needs, build up their retirement funds, or simply to have money for rainy days. Instead of looking at what other people have, you will likely be more content if you shift your focus to your own priorities and the more important things that can bring real and lasting happiness in life.

Lessons from the Pro

"Be more concerned with your character than your reputation, because your character is what you really are, while your reputation is merely what others think you are."

John Wooden
Basketball Coach/Player

LESSONS ON CREDIT CARDS

Lesson #19:
Credit Cards Are Beneficial When Used Responsibly

In *Finance 101*, you learned about credit cards. **Credit** is an agreement between a borrower and a lender/creditor in which the borrower gets something valuable and promises to pay for it in the future. When you use a credit card to make a purchase, you become a **borrower**. The creditor pays the store for the items that you bought. As a borrower, you are required to pay back the creditor in full for every dollar that you borrowed. That means none of those things you bought with a credit card is free!

You might be asking why use a credit card if you will need to pay back everything you owe anyway? Why not just use cash and avoid the risk of overspending? It is true that credit cards can lead to overspending, but using a credit card also has many benefits when used responsibly. Among the benefits are:

1. A credit card makes paying convenient, especially when you do not have enough cash in your wallet. Credit cards are also very useful when dealing with financial emergencies or unplanned expenses.

2. You can easily track your expenses. The credit card companies will send you monthly statements detailing all the purchases you made. Many credit card companies also offer quarterly and yearly spending summaries, which can be helpful when you make plans and budget.

3. A credit card helps you establish a good credit history and rating, which will become very valuable when you apply for bigger loans in the future, such as student loans, car loans, and home loans. Of course, a good credit rating is only possible when you properly manage your credit card.

4. You can get rewards and cash back when you use a credit card. **Cash back** is the money sent back to

you after using the credit card to make purchases. When you have a good credit standing, credit card companies will compete for your business and offer you rewards, including cash back. Sometimes, credit card companies offer as much as 3 percent cash back. This means for every $100 you spend using the credit card, they will give you $3 back. If cash back is offered, using a credit card to buy stuff that you will need to purchase anyway makes a lot of sense.

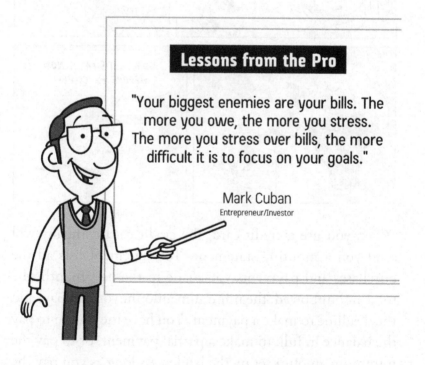

Lessons from the Pro

"Your biggest enemies are your bills. The more you owe, the more you stress. The more you stress over bills, the more difficult it is to focus on your goals."

Mark Cuban
Entrepreneur/Investor

Lesson #20:
Never Miss Your
Credit Card Payments

When you use a credit card, the credit card company will send you a monthly statement. The statement lists all the purchases and payments you made in the past month, the total amount owed, the minimum amount you can pay, and the deadline to make a payment. You have the option to pay the balance in full, to make a partial payment, or to pay the minimum amount set by the lender. As long as you pay the entire amount before the due date, you will not be charged any interest. **Interest** is money charged by the banking or credit institute for using their money. If you pay only a partial or minimum amount, the credit card company will start charging you interest for the remaining unpaid balance.

A good guideline to follow with credit cards is to spend only up to what you can afford to pay back immediately. Credit card companies usually charge a very high interest rate for the unpaid balance, and the interest can easily become a burden when it piles up. Unless there is an emergency or an urgent need to buy a certain item that cannot be delayed, you should consider waiting until you can afford to make that purchase.

In the event that you cannot pay the entire balance, you still need to pay at least the minimum amount set by the credit card company. As a borrower, you have an obligation to make regular monthly payments. Failure to make timely payments on your credit card obligations can result in unpleasant consequences.

When a credit card payment is missed, the creditors will start charging late fees on top of the interest. They will send letters reminding the borrower that a payment is due immediately. Sometimes, they will contact the borrower directly to remind him or her that a payment was missed. If the borrower continues to ignore the calls or letters and fails to make payments, the creditor will take more drastic measures to get their money back. This includes reporting the borrower to the credit bureaus and sending your account to a debt collection agency.

Failing to pay your credit card is not only costly, but it can also affect your career and your reputation. Many employers check on credit reports when they screen job applicants. If they see that you have missed a number of your payment obligations, they might consider giving the job to another applicant who has shown a higher level of maturity and responsibility. If you need to rent an apartment someday, the landlord can also check your credit report. The landlord will likely hand over the keys of the apartment to someone who has consistently made timely payments on their obligations.

You have learned that a credit card can be a great tool that can help you manage your money and build a good credit history. Having a credit card can be exciting, but you have to know and understand the consequences of overspending and not making payments on time. You need to be on top of your responsibilities all the time, as mismanaged credit can be costly and damaging to your credibility.

LESSONS ON SAVING AND INVESTING

Lesson #21:
Learn to Delay Gratification

Delayed gratification is the act of putting off something fun or enjoyable today in order to gain something better or more rewarding in the future. An example of delayed gratification is choosing to study as opposed to playing video games the night before an exam. Playing video games is fun, but you also know that studying for your exams helps you get higher grades, which is more rewarding and gratifying in the long run. However, the temptation and the pleasure of instant gratification can sometimes be very difficult to resist.

In finance, delayed gratification is the act of putting off the things you want to buy now so you can have something better in the future. When you save your money, you are basically delaying gratification because you are putting a hold on spending.

Delaying gratification can be a big challenge to a lot of people. It is not easy to say no to things that you desire. You need strong willpower and foresight to delay gratification. **Foresight** is the ability to think ahead and prepare for the future.

When you start to make a budget, your plans may include short-term and long-term goals. Short-term goals are something that you want to achieve in one year or less, whereas long-term goals are those that you want to accomplish in several years. An example of a short-term goal is saving money to buy a computer for your school needs. With delayed gratification, you might have to resist upgrading your phone when there is no need for it, or you might have to put a limit on eating out so that you can save extra money that you can add to your computer fund.

Getting a college degree is a good example of a long-term goal. In general, people with college degrees earn significantly more in their lifetime than people without college degrees. However, going through college can be costly, especially if you decide to go to a prestigious private school. Although scholarships and student loans may be available, delaying instant gratification by starting a college fund is something that you can do at a young age. Although you can use your money now for something cool and fun, you can also save some of it to help yourself achieve that goal of getting a college degree.

Lessons from the Pro

"The ability to discipline yourself to delay gratification in the short term in order to enjoy greater rewards in the long term, is the indispensable prerequisite for success."

Brian Tracy
Motivational Speaker/Author

Lesson #22:
Use the Power of Compound Interest

Do you remember the formula we learned in *Finance 101* on how to compute the amount of interest your money can earn?

Interest = Principal x Rate x Time

To review, **interest** is the payment for the use of money. If you deposit money in the bank, your money earns interest because you are letting the bank use your money for their business. You earn more interest if any of the three components (principal, rate, time) gets bigger. This means the more money you put into savings (principal), or the higher the interest rate, or the longer the money is invested (time), the more interest you earn.

Generally, you have no control over the rate because this component is determined by different market forces beyond your control. Although the interest rate may slightly differ from one bank to another, the overall interest rate will be the same across the nation, and it may change over time depending on the condition of the economy. However, the good news is that you can control the other two components. You decide how much money you will save and invest. You also decide when to start saving and investing and how long you will keep your money invested.

There are two types of interest: simple interest and compound interest. **Simple interest** is the interest that is applied only to the original principal. For example, when you deposit $1,000 in a bank that pays 5 percent interest per year, your money will earn $50 ($1,000 x 5 percent x 1 year) in simple interest.

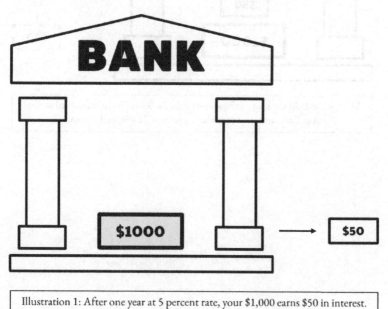

Illustration 1: After one year at 5 percent rate, your $1,000 earns $50 in interest.

Now suppose you decide to keep both the original $1000 and the $50 interest in the bank. When this happens, the interest you earn will be added to your bank account. This means at the start of the second year, you will have $1,050 because the $50 you earned last year is added to the bank.

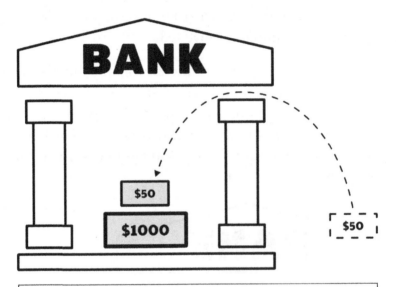

Illustration 2: At the start of the second year, the $50 in interest is added to your bank account, and you'll have a total of $1,050 in the bank.

Because the interest you earned has been added to your bank account, it will also earn interest. Assuming that the rate remains at 5 percent, the $50 will earn an interest of $2.50 on its own, while your original $1,000 will continue to earn $50. At the end of the year, your money will earn a total of $52.50 in interest.

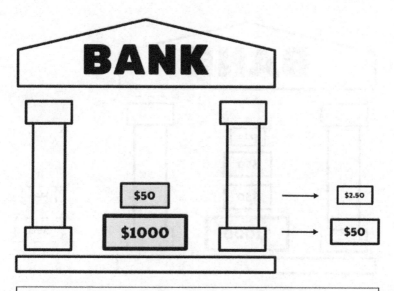

Illustration 3: At the end of the second year, the $50 made $2.50 in interest, while the $1,000 made another $50 in interest. The total interest earned is $52.50.

Suppose you continue to keep your money in the bank. At the start of the third year, the interest you earned in the previous year will be added again to the principal. This means that at the start of the third year, your total money in the bank will amount to $1,102.50 ($1,000 + $50 +$50 + $2.50).

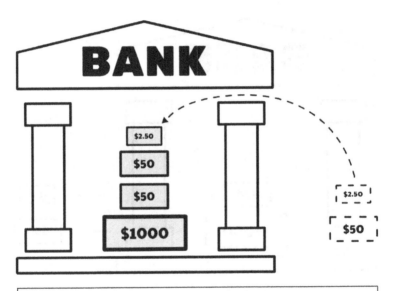

Illustration 4: At the start of the third year, the $50 and the $2.50 in interest are added to your bank account, and you'll have a total of $1,102.50 in the bank.

Then, at the end of third year, all the money you have in the bank will earn interest. Assuming that the rate remains at 5 percent, your money in the bank will earn $55.12. See the breakdown of this amount in Illustration 5.

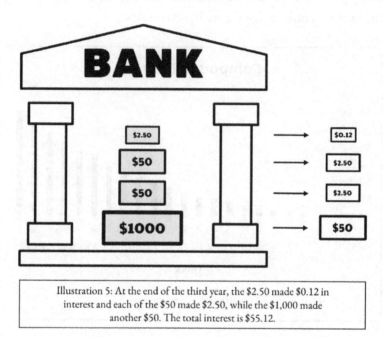

Illustration 5: At the end of the third year, the $2.50 made $0.12 in interest and each of the $50 made $2.50, while the $1,000 made another $50. The total interest is $55.12.

Do you see the difference in the interest that was earned in the first year ($50) versus the second year ($52.50) and the third year ($55.12)? Your money is making more every year because of compound interest. In a nutshell, **compound interest** is the interest that is applied to the original principal and all the interests that are earned and added to the principal. In other words, you can make extra money on top of the interest you made! Compounding can create a snowball effect because your original money plus the income you earn grow together.

From this example, it may appear that the interest you earned is not that big. But if you look at the next graph which will show how much your money can earn over a long period of time, compound interest will have a huge impact to your savings and investments.

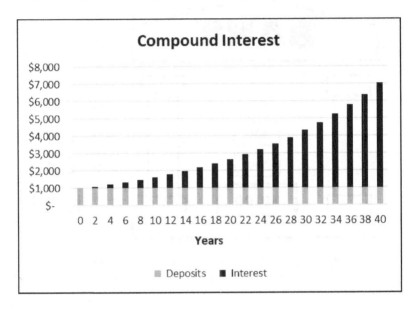

With compound interest, your money can make more money every year because you earn interest on interest. Assuming that your money continues to earn 5 percent every year, the $1,000 money you saved and invested will double in about 14 years and it will be worth more than $7,000 after 40 years. Isn't that amazing? Compound interest is a powerful saving tool that can help you reach your financial goals. Even the famous scientist Albert Einstein was fascinated by compound interest, and he described it as the "Eighth Wonder of the World."

Lesson #23:
Put Time on Your Side

Kids like you are in a great position to greatly benefit from the power of compounding interest because you have more time than adults to make your money grow. The sooner you start saving and investing, the higher the reward you will reap. When you start to save and invest early, you are giving your money more time to grow. The power of compounding can help your money earn more when you give it more time to grow.

To help you understand how time affects your money, let us illustrate how saving early can work well for a young person versus saving at a later time.

Ben started to save in 2020, whereas George was happy spending all the money he got. Ben saved $50/month, which he put in a bank that pays 5% compounding interest. After 20 years, George finally realized the importance of saving for the future, so he also started to save $50/month and put it at the same bank that pays 5% interest. Both of them continued to save $50/month for another 20 years. This is where their investments stand after 40 years:

As you can see, Ben was able to save twice the amount of money than George ($24,000 vs. $12,000). What is more amazing is that Ben's investment made a lot more money than George's investment ($48,480 vs. $7,840) because Ben utilized the power of time and compounding interest. Ben is in a much better financial position, all because he started **saving and investing earlier** than George. When you combine the power of time and compounding interest, you will have a more secured future waiting for you!

Many people see the importance of saving, yet some are not willing to save. Oftentimes, people's income increases over time, but they also change their lifestyle and spend more, resulting in no savings. Unfortunately, you cannot be financially secure without a willingness to save. Saving is very important because the future can be unpredictable. Having some funds set aside for future use, especially for emergencies, can be a big source of relief when an unexpected expense or an emergency situation arises.

When the coronavirus hit the world in early 2020, many people were caught off guard by this pandemic. Millions of people lost their jobs because all of a sudden, the economy and businesses slowed down. Those who lost their jobs with little savings were unable to support the needs of their families. Some of them had to line up at food banks. It was heartbreaking to see that people who could afford to buy fancy cars and expensive clothes prior to the pandemic became jobless and were unable to pay for their necessities because of the lack of savings.

While you are still young, you should develop the good habit of saving and investing. It's very prudent to save at least a third of any money you earn or receive and put it to work for you. When you carry this habit of saving regularly into adulthood, saving will not be as difficult as it seems because you already have a good system in place and the discipline to make smarter choices.

LESSONS ON PROTECTING YOUR MONEY, PROPERTY, AND REPUTATION

Lesson #24:
Don't Store Your Savings in a Shoebox

Some people, kids and adults alike, store their money in a shoebox, under a mattress, inside a sock drawer, or in some secret location in the house. Some people feel that their money is safer when they can see it. Others keep their money at home so they can easily access it when needed.

Although having cash at home is important so you have money for small purchases and emergencies, storing all of your savings at home may not be a very smart idea. The money at home is at risk of being lost, stolen, or forgotten. Any house or apartment can catch fire and burn down. If a house burns down, all the money you have stored in a shoebox could burn with it. Similarly, bad weather like a hurricane, a tornado, or a flood can devastate a home and everything inside. Also, money in a house can be stolen by robbers or by a person you know who got tempted to steal your stash of cash.

Besides the physical loss, the money stored at home is losing value over time. Do you remember inflation from *Finance 101*? **Inflation** is the general increase in prices of goods and services. Generally, the costs of goods and services go up every year. This means the money you have today inside your house can buy less in a couple of years because the prices will have gone higher.

Suppose $10 can buy a movie ticket today. If you save that $10 in a shoebox and pull it out in five years, it probably won't be able the buy a movie ticket. By that time, the cost of the movie ticket will likely be higher.

If you want to protect your money and make it grow, you'll probably want to bring your money to a savings bank. Banks store money and other valuables inside a fireproof vault that can withstand most natural calamities. And even if your bank is robbed, like the ones you might have seen in movies, the money deposited in a bank is insured by the government up to a certain amount ($250,000 in the United States). Likewise, the money you have in a bank earns interest. Your money is growing and can possibly offset the effects of inflation. Even if the bank's interest rate is low, any growth of your money is better than zero growth when it is stored in a shoebox.

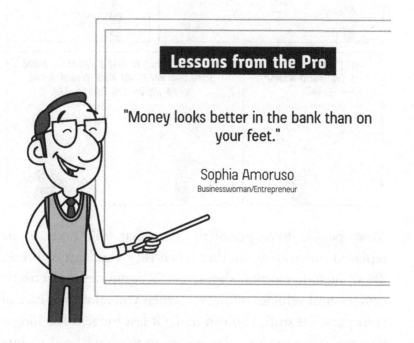

Lessons from the Pro

"Money looks better in the bank than on your feet."

Sophia Amoruso
Businesswoman/Entrepreneur

Lesson #25:
Take Good Care of Your Personal Stuff and Make It Last

Most people have personal items that will need to be replaced one way or another when they wear out or break. These include clothes, shoes, sports equipment, electronic devices, and vehicles. However, when you take good care of your personal stuff, you can make it last longer. The longer you are able to use it, the less often you will need to buy replacements or the fewer trips you need to make to the repair shop. Prolonging the usage of your personal stuff easily translates to more savings for you in the long run. When you are able to use the things you own for a longer period of time, you are getting more value for your money. Even if you received the item as a gift and you did not use your own money to obtain that item, taking care of your personal stuff is beneficial because you are able to minimize your expenses.

There are many simple things that you can do to help prolong the life of your personal stuff, but oftentimes, you tend to overlook or ignore them because they seem too simple. For example, you can prevent shrinkage and fading of your clothes when you wash them inside out using cold water. Your shoes will last longer when you keep them clean, dry, and smelling fresh. For your computers and laptops, you can reduce the risk of overheating when you regularly clean and de-clog vents and ports to maintain good airflow. When not in use, storing your personal stuff in a clean and organized area is also an easy way to keep it in good condition. You can easily find more information online on other ways to extend the life of your personal stuff.

Taking good care of your stuff also means protecting it from getting misplaced, lost, or stolen. Sometimes, unfortunate events happen that cause you to lose your personal belongings. You might have accidentally left your stuff in a public area, or someone unscrupulously stole your phone or your new pair of shoes. If the item you lost is something you need for school or work, you don't have much choice but to buy a replacement. This unplanned spending can strain your budget. To avoid this, remember to always secure all your personal belongings, and never leave your valuable items exposed to potential thieves.

Lesson #26:
Protect Your Personal Information

Personal information is any information that is used to identify and locate an individual. Examples of personal information are someone's name, home address, Social Security number, birthdate, driver's license number, bank account numbers, and credit card numbers. Most of this personal information is required when someone is opening a new account in schools, libraries, and business organizations. When applying for a job or any form of credit, like credit cards and car loans, the applicant has to prove his or her identity by providing personal information and identification documents.

Although the technology that protects personal information keeps improving, thieves and cybercriminals are also getting smarter. They can find ways to steal personal information and use that to create fake accounts. They can also steal your credit card information and use it to shop.

When the fake accounts or the stolen credit cards are used, the innocent victims end up being chased by the creditors for payments. In most cases, the fraudulent charges will be erased once the victim reports that his or her identity or credit card has been stolen and used inappropriately. However, the hassle involved with clearing one's name and identity can be stressful and time consuming.

To avoid becoming a victim of identity theft, you should not give your personal information to someone you don't know or you don't trust. You should avoid responding to unsolicited requests for personal information from emails, pop-up ads, text messages, phone calls, letters, or someone showing up at your front door. They might be scammers who are trying to trick you. You should also be very careful downloading email attachments from someone you don't know, installing unnecessary apps on your phone, and opening new online accounts, especially when the credibility of the app or the website is questionable.

Cyber criminals can obtain your personal information by breaking into your online accounts. Most online accounts such as emails, social network accounts, online stores, gaming sites, and online banking accounts contain much of the subscribers' personal information. One of the easiest ways for the hackers to break in is by guessing the passwords. The simpler the password is, the easier it is to guess and access the account. On the other hand, having a strong password makes it more difficult to crack.

To fortify your defense against cybercriminals, you should make your passwords long and complex, but personal, so they will be easy for you to remember. Passwords should contain uppercase and lowercase letters and numbers in combination with special characters, such as exclamation points, parentheses, percent signs, and "at" signs. (Example: !Lov3myC@T). Also, you should not use the same password for different accounts or devices because a single episode of a break-in can give the hacker access to many of your online accounts or devices.

Lessons from the Pro

"If you put a key under the mat for the cops, a burglar can find it, too. Criminals are using every technology tool at their disposal to hack into people's accounts. If they know there's a key hidden somewhere, they won't stop until they find it."

Tim Cook
Business Executive/Philanthropist

Lesson #27:
Online Actions Have Consequences

Online communication has become a way of life. Many people around the world spend many hours on their computers, tablets, and phones browsing and communicating through social networking platforms like Facebook, Instagram, and Snapchat. The internet has made it easy and efficient for people to share messages, thoughts, opinions, jokes, milestones, photos, and videos.

Online communication can help a person connect with others, but anyone who has access to this tool needs to realize the huge responsibility that comes with it. Posting statements, pictures, or videos that are damaging to a reputation or hurtful to someone can cause problems that can negatively impact your schooling, career, safety, and even your financial standing.

Because of the vast amount of information available on the internet, many employers, recruiters, school admission officers, and even academic advisors are checking the internet and doing their research before hiring or accepting applicants. Posting pictures and videos of you doing something illegal and embarrassing or offending another person or an institution can take away your chances of getting into good schools or landing your dream job. You might even get in trouble with the school or the local authorities for incriminating photos and false information you posted. A bad post can result in school expulsion or jail time.

You have to remember that your online actions have consequences that can possibly haunt you for a long time. Even if you realized you made a mistake and deleted a bad post quickly, there may still be a screenshot saved somewhere that can be reshared online. Even the private messages you sent to someone through the internet or as a text message can eventually become a part of the public forum when reshared. Unfortunately, you may never be able to run away from the things you post online. Therefore, always think first and use good judgment before posting anything online.

LESSONS ON MONEY AND LIFE PRINCIPLES

Lesson #28:
Be Thankful for What You Have

Even though you do not have all the things you want, you probably own a few items that other kids can only wish for. Many children do not experience the same privileges and comforts that you have. Their families may be experiencing challenges that hinder them from getting the things they need. Some children even have to give up school in order to help their families make a living. When you realize that some children are not as fortunate as you are, you don't have to feel guilty for what you have, but you can definitely be thankful for all the blessings that you receive.

There are many reasons to be thankful. You can be thankful for the food on the table, the clothes you wear, and all the material items you have. You can also be thankful for the home that keeps you safe and warm, and for all the privileges of being able to surf the internet, watch TV, or play video games. However, beyond the personal material possessions, you can be more thankful for the people who make your life brighter. Be thankful to your parents and your family who care for you, to your teachers who help you grow smarter and stronger, and to your friends, mentors, schoolmates, and neighbors who are making big and small positive impacts in your life.

Saying thank you to people around you should never be taken for granted. When you say thank you, you show your appreciation for what they have done or who they have been. You acknowledge their actions or their great personalities, and you let them know how important they are to you. It is a simple but effective way to show love and respect. Bear in mind that people feel good when someone makes them feel loved and appreciated.

Being thankful does not only make people see you in a positive light, but it also makes you better in handling your money and finances. When you choose to be thankful, you will have a better appreciation of the things you have. Appreciating your belongings will make you feel happier and more content. Being thankful for what you have can help you ignore and resist the constant ads that tempt you to spend more. It also prevents you from feeling envious or resentful when you see other people having better stuff than you do. By being thankful, you can realize how blessed and fortunate you are to be living a wonderful life, no matter how simple or how fancy the things you have.

Lessons from the Pro

"Be thankful for what you have; you'll end up having more. If you concentrate on what you don't have, you will never, ever have enough."

Oprah Winfrey
Television Host/Philanthropist

Lesson #29:
Money Is Not the Only Thing That Can Make You Rich

Shoes: $150

Phone: $799

Having fun with family and friends: Priceless

People often associate being rich with having lots of money, expensive cars, fancy toys, and big houses. Money can buy lots of things, but not everything has a price tag. There are many wonderful things in this world that can make a person rich and happy in different ways, even with little or no money.

Think of a time when you were playing and having fun with your friends. If you have friends whom you can laugh with, cry with, and grow up with, then you are rich because you have true friends. Though money can buy services like drivers to take you to school, trainers to get you in good shape, or a nanny to take care of you when you are sick, money cannot buy real friendship.

Think of the wonderful times you have had with your family sharing food and laughter over dinner, or enjoying a walk at the park, or attending sports and religious services together. If you have a family that cares for you, then you are rich because you have a family with whom you can share your joys and sorrows with, and on whom you can count for support through the good times and the bad.

Think of the games you have played, the sports and events you have participated in, the trips you have taken, the projects you have made, the books you have read, the movies you have watched, and the countless hours you have listened to and learned from your teachers, parents, and peers. With these experiences, you are rich in wisdom and beautiful memories that you can always cherish.

Think of a time when you helped someone in your own little way, and you did not ask for anything in return. Think of the times you decided to follow rules not because it was the easiest way but because you knew it was the right thing to do. When you do good deeds, you are rich because you have a great character. A reputation of great character cannot be bought with money. It can only be earned by being kind, helpful, and respectful.

Lesson #30:
Sharing Is Caring

Sharing one's wealth is a very noble act, but many people are unwilling to do it. It is probably because people know how hard it is to earn or make money, and it may seem irrational to give up some of that money to let someone else benefit from it. But sharing makes a lot of sense because when you are generous, you are making a positive impact on your community. Many people who share their wealth and give back to the community also find a higher purpose and greater happiness in their lives.

There are many people in your community who may not be as fortunate as you are. Some families may be experiencing financial difficulties due to losing a parent or a loved one. Some might have lost their jobs. Others may have health conditions that prevent them from working or supporting themselves.

Although you may not completely resolve their problems, you can do something to help them get through their difficulties and make them feel good and cared for. One such act of generosity is donating to charities and religious institutions. **Charities** are organizations that provide help and assistance to the needy. There are different charities and religion-based organizations in your community that are helping the homeless, the families who cannot afford to buy food, the children who are lost or neglected, and the elderly people who need support. By donating to charities or religious institutions, you are helping them in their missions to improve the lives of many people in need.

There are charities that accept non-monetary donations, such as clothes, shoes, toys, books, canned goods, and school supplies. Those charities either distribute the donated goods directly to the needy or sell the donated goods to raise money for their missions. Even though you might think that the item or the money you donate is not much, remember that when your donation is pooled together with the other donations, it can become a powerful force big enough to make an impact.

When you don't have the capacity to donate money or possessions to your community, you can also be generous with your time and talent as a volunteer. You can start by serving as a mentor for another kid who is struggling with schoolwork or sports. As you grow up, you can help organize fundraisers and service projects or promote campaigns or public events. You can do some work for animal shelters, charities, food banks, and religious institutions, even for a short period of time. There are many ways you can serve as a volunteer in the community. You can check with your schools or your local religious institutions or charities on the different ways you can serve as a volunteer.

When it comes to sharing, you have many choices on how you can do this. But no matter what form of sharing and giving you choose, being generous can be a rewarding experience as you can make a positive impact in your community, and in most likelihood, a big difference in someone's life.

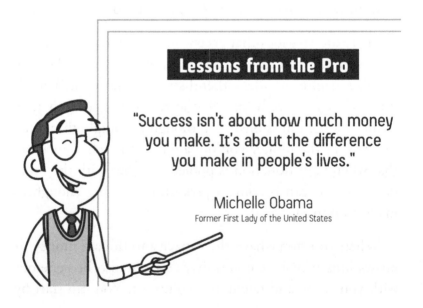

Lessons from the Pro

"Success isn't about how much money you make. It's about the difference you make in people's lives."

Michelle Obama
Former First Lady of the United States

Afterword

"SOMEONE IS SITTING IN THE SHADE TODAY BECAUSE SOMEONE PLANTED A TREE A LONG TIME AGO."

—WARREN BUFFET

Trees are vital. They keep the air clean and the ecosystems healthy. They provide many types of fruits and nuts, wood for building, and pulp to make paper. During hot weather, trees can provide you shade to cool you down. But big trees don't just magically appear in your yard. If you want a tree, you have to dig up the soil, plant the seeds, water the area regularly, and nurture the sapling as it slowly grows bigger and stronger over time.

The way to build a successful financial future is similar to how you grow a tree. You have to use the power of planning and planting ahead and do some legwork, too. To create wealth and secure your future, it is vital for you to plan and make a budget, learn good financial skills and practice them, become consistent with saving a portion of your earnings, and prudently make your money grow over time.

Although the future is unpredictable, you can prepare yourself for what is to come to the best of your abilities. Those who plan well and plant the seeds early in their lives reap bountiful rewards later on. Keep on learning, spend and invest your money wisely, and make good judgments while you are still young. When you grow up, you will enjoy the rewards of your hard work and smart choices.

It has been a pleasure to have you again in this class. Please stay safe and strong, and good luck with your amazing journey! Until we see each other again....

References

Burkholder, Steve. *I Want More Pizza: Real World Money Skills for High School, College, and Beyond.* Overcome Publishing LLC, 2017.

Butler, Tamsen. *The Complete Guide to Personal Finance for Teenagers and College Students, 2ⁿᵈ Edition.* Florida: Atlantic Publishing Group, 2016.

Clifton, Jacob. "Is It Worth It to Splurge on Name Brands?" Howstuffworks.com. Accessed May 3, 2020. https://money. howstuffworks.com/personal-finance/budgeting/is-it-worth-it-to-splurge-on-name-brands.htm.

"Dealing with Peer Pressure." Kidshealth.org. Accessed August 2, 2020. https://kidshealth.org/en/kids/peer-pressure.html

Irby, Latoya. "Tips for Teaching Your Child About Using a Credit Card." Thebalance.com. Accessed July 5, 2020. https://www.thebalance.com/teach-your-child-about-credit-cards-960193

Kane, Libby. "Loads of Americans Literally Hide Money Under the Mattress — Here's Why It's a Terrible Idea." Businessinsider.com. February 11, 2015. Accessed July 12, 2020. https://www.businessinsider.com/americans-hide-money-under-the-mattress-2015-2.

Lieber, Ron. *The Opposite of Spoiled: Raising Kids Who Are Grounded, Generous, and Smart About Money.* New York: Harper Collins Publisher, 2015.

Moss, Wes. "Should You Buy New or Used Items?" Thebalance. com. May 17, 2020. Accessed July 21, 2020. https://www. thebalance.com/should-you-buy-new-or-used-4054264.

"Net Cetera Chatting with Kids About Being Online." FTC. gov. Accessed June 13, 2020. https://www.consumer.ftc. gov/sites/www.consumer.ftc.gov/files/netcetera_2018.pdf

Reid, Holly D. *Teach Your Child to Fish: Five Money Habits Every Child Should Master.* Georgia: The Master Playbook, 2016.

Scearce, Jane. "25 Unnecessary Wastes of Money You Don't Think About." Lifehack.org. Accessed July 21, 2020. https:// www.lifehack.org/articles/money/25-unnecessary-wastes-money-you-dont-think-about.html.

Siegel, Cary. *Why Didn't They Teach Me This in School? 99 Personal Money Management Principles.* South Carolina: CreateSpace Independent Publishing, 2018.

Smith, Kurt. "Why You Shouldn't Try to Keep Up with the Joneses." Pyschcentral.com. July 8, 2018. Accessed June 7, 2020. https://psychcentral.com/blog/why-you-shouldnt-try-to-keep-up-with-the-joneses.

Yarrow, Kit. "12 Ways to Stop Wasting Money and Take Control of Your Stuff." Money.com. November 20, 2014. Accessed May 14, 2020. https://money.com/overspending-overconsumption-stuff.

Made in the USA
Las Vegas, NV
15 September 2024

95305729R10066